CHANGE YOUR MINDSET WITH LOFTY QUESTIONS

YOUR 7-DAY CHALLENGE

EMILY WATSON

CONTENTS

Introduction

Thank you for committing to seven days in your life to become a better version of yourself. The Mindset Reset Challenge is a 7-day challenge that prompts you to start your day with self-reflection, some practical tips and a set of lofty questions that focus on improving your mindset about specific topics in your life. It helps you get into a "winning" state of mind by focusing on self-esteem, confidence, positivity, money, health, abundance and gratitude.

The duration of the challenge is seven days for two main reasons: 1) it's short enough to be manageable yet long enough to have an impact, and 2) each day focuses on one specific aspect of mindset improvement, allowing you to focus on one thing at a time rather than trying to keep track of multiple goals at once. The structure of the challenge is designed so that each day's lofty questions build upon the previous ones.

No matter how talented or intelligent someone is, they will never be able to reach their full potential if they don't have a healthy mindset. Mindset is the most crucial thing in our lives. It dramatically impacts what we achieve and how we feel about ourselves. Most people have heard of the "fresh start" mentality—how you can take advantage of a new year to clean up your life, or maybe even start one. However, a less common type of fresh start has the same power to change your life as the new year: changing your mindset.

Many people are unaware of their mindset but can change it with simple tricks. One of these tricks is asking lofty questions to change the way you think. A lofty question is a question-and-affirmation method that makes you feel good and changes your perspective on an issue. The popular learning platform, *Mind Valley*, made lofty questions more known and is a new way to learn about personal transformation. Why are lofty questions helpful? A lofty question stretches you to think beyond your usual scope of perception. Its purpose is to create a paradigm shift so that you see the world differently. A lofty question makes you go, "hmm...I've never thought about it that way!"

Your subconscious mind is more likely to change in a good way when you ask yourself big questions. The questions help you get out of emotional ruts and make changes work better for you. They give your subconscious mind a chance to create creative answers to your questions and help you use your intuition, get new ideas, and change your focus. When your subconscious mind answers these questions leads to more good things happening in your life.

I designed the 7-day challenge to help you self-reflect on your self-esteem, confidence, positivity, money, health, abundance and gratitude each day for seven days and what all these mean for a successful life. Each day also provides some practical exercises you can implement in your life immediately and concludes with 15 lofty questions. Because your subconscious mind always wants answers to questions, you will attract changes in your life to answer these questions. As an additional option, you can also practice a mudra (ritual gesture) while asking these questions.

Making the most of this challenge

The things in life that we most desire are often the things we least appreciate. Looking at how we live and treat ourselves, it's clear that constant change is the only truly consistent thing. It's essential to see this fact, as it can help demonstrate what matters to us and how we can become better people.

Remember breaking a bad habit can be a difficult task. It can be even more challenging when you don't realise the damage the pattern is causing. Habits tend to reinforce themselves. You do them until your brain learns how to do them and doesn't have to spend any energy or resources thinking about it. Breaking that habit means putting in the effort and energy that your brain will have to expend, which makes it more likely that you will give up before you succeed.

To make the most of this 7-day challenge, you must set aside at least 30 minutes per day for each of the topics I address daily. Only focus on one day at a time and resist the temptation to move on to another day on the same day. In this way, you will benefit most.

We all know the physical benefits of getting enough sleep and exercise, but there are also mental health benefits. Your brain is like any other muscle in your body—the more you use it, the stronger it gets. When you're not using it, you're letting it rest. If you're spending time relaxing your brain, why not do so in a way that helps you mentally which is the aim of this challenge.

Are you ready to join this challenge? But it is important to first get to know how your mind works.

Getting To Know Your Mind

The mind is everything that makes you who you are. It's your brain, your thoughts, and how you feel. Your brain consists of neurons, which communicate with each other to make you do and think things and also feel something.

If you want an example of how the brain works, think of a computer. A computer's hardware is like the brain's neurons. The software is like the mind—all of its programs are what make a computer do what it does. The mind then can be thought of as a program that runs on top of the hardware (brain).

What if you could change your mind, feelings or thoughts? You can! If you really want to know what someone else feels like, imagine yourself in the same situation and imagine how you would feel. If you can't imagine it, try reading a book or watching a movie that has something similar in it. For example, it can be beneficial to think about other people's situations before they happen. You will then be ready for them and know how to react effectively when they happen to you.

How does your mind affect you?

Your mind allows you to sense, think, reason, experience emotions, and remember. It consists of your brain and nervous system that carries information between your body and the brain. Your mind has many functions. It processes sensory input from your five senses (touch, sight, hearing, taste and smell) and information you receive by thinking. It also controls your thoughts and memories. You use your mind to make decisions about things in your environment (for example, what to do when you see a dog). From these decisions, you take action. Your actions can result in voluntary behaviour (for example, answering a question) or involuntary (for example, a knee-jerk reaction). Your actions can also be unintentional (for example, an accident).

It's hard to argue with the notion that our minds are influential. We all know from experience that when we're in a good mood and feeling optimistic, things tend to go better than when we're in a bad mood and feeling pessimistic. That's because the mind profoundly affects your body and your circumstances.

But how, exactly? And what can you do about it?

Some of the most exciting research in neuroscience has been exploring this question. In studies examining brain activity and blood flow, scientists have verified that positive thoughts can release neurotransmitters such as dopamine, oxytocin, and serotonin. These chemicals influence everything from sleep patterns to pain sensitivity—and even how fast your heart beats. They also play an essential role in your ability to concentrate or plan, ultimately affecting your work or study performance.

The list of positive effects doesn't stop there. There is evidence that positive emotions support long-term happiness and overall well-being by supporting relationships and improving your immune system, among other things. Each time you feel happy or sad, or angry, you activate neurons in specific areas of your brain and release chemical reactions throughout your entire body.

There are two types of people in this world: those who think that their actions affect their lives and those who believe that their life conditions influence how they act. Many scientists fall into the camp of the latter—they say that genetics and psychology are what determine our behaviour.

Your conscious and subconscious mind

Did you know that you have both a conscious and subconscious mind? But what are the differences between the subconscious and conscious mind and how can you use them to your advantage? The human brain is an incredibly complex system that is still not fully understood by experts. However, the general structure of the brain consists of two main parts, namely the conscious mind and the subconscious mind.

The conscious mind is the part of our mental activity that we are aware of and can control. We use this part of the mind to think, feel, remember and imagine. When we see or hear something, the information is picked up by our sensory organs and sent to the brain, where the conscious mind processes it and stores it in memory. The same goes for when we touch, taste or smell something.

On the other hand, the subconscious mind is the part of our consciousness responsible for processing all the information we are exposed to. It is also the part of us that analyses and decides how to react to these stimuli. The subconscious mind takes in all the information and stimuli around us but doesn't process everything consciously. Instead, it keeps much of this out of our conscious awareness and deals with it under the radar. If you want to understand how this works, think about how you learn new things—you aren't constantly analysing every detail. Still, instead, you pick up on little things throughout your experience. Maybe a particular shape or colour triggers your memory: when you see that shape again, you have an 'ah-ha' moment and realise where you saw it before. Over time, you build up associations between different things until you can fill in the entire picture without thinking about it or analysing each detail.

This same thing happens with many other kinds of stimuli, including what you hear, smell, and feel. For example, if someone walks into your office wearing cologne that reminds you of a particular person, your mind will make an association between that scent and person.

When you're dreaming, your subconscious mind is at work. In a dream, you may be running from a monster or trying to fly—these things may seem real, but they're all happening in your subconscious. The dream is produced by the millions of tiny cells firing billions of electrical charges at each other in your brain. The cells are connected by synapses communicating these electrical charges from one cell to the next. In this way, they form neural pathways. These neural pathways include what we know as our habits and behaviours. These pathways are stored in the subconscious part of our brain because they're not directly related to our survival daily. The conscious mind helps us consciously make decisions and control our actions. It also allows us to plan and organise. For example, when driving a car, our conscious mind is responsible for overseeing the pedals, steering wheel, and gear shift. At the same time, our subconscious handles everything else behind the scenes (like keeping us on the road). Our subconscious mind gives us much more freedom and power than if we had to consciously direct every little muscle movement that

keeps us on the road! Now imagine what could happen if we could speak to our subconscious minds.

Let's start with the 7-day challenge next. Are you ready? Remember to only focus on one aspect per day for best results.

Day 1: Dealing With Your Self-Esteem

Day 1 of this challenge is all about working on your self-esteem. Low self-esteem can affect your quality of life and prevent you from living a happy, fulfilling life.

First, let's define what self-esteem is. Self-esteem is an elusive concept. Understanding self-esteem can sometimes be challenging and even more difficult to achieve. There are different methods for attaining self-esteem, but it comes from within at its root. It is essential to note the difference between self-confidence and self-esteem. While they are similar, they are not the same thing. The best definition of self-esteem is that it is your own opinion of yourself which differs from self-confidence because it does not include how others feel about you.

Low self-esteem means the opinion you have of yourself and the worth you place on yourself are lacking. On the other hand, if you have a high level of self-esteem, you value your opinions, like your personality and physical appearance. You are more confident in what you do and how you do it. And when you're more confident in your actions, it makes you feel better about who you are.

The most obvious explanation for why good self-esteem is essential is because it will make you feel good about yourself. Focusing on things that make you happy makes you more likely to be satisfied. Psychology Today explains that "people with high self-esteem experience more positive and fewer negative emotions," making your life happier.

Secondly, good self-esteem can help prevent or end destructive behaviours. If you do not like yourself, you are more likely to engage in risky or unhealthy behaviour such as drug abuse, addiction, smoking, or eating disorders. Having good self-esteem can encourage healthy behaviour such as exercising and eating right. Engaging in these activities has been linked to a longer life and better quality of life.

Lastly, having good self-esteem will help you achieve your goals. If you have faith in yourself, you will be more confident in your abilities and what you can achieve in life. There are many ways to improve your self-esteem; therapy is one way to work through personal issues that may affect how you perceive yourself.

Who has high self-esteem?

Anyone can have self-esteem! It's not just a trait that some people have, and others don't. Everyone can work on their self-esteem. Some people might be born with great genetics or parents who give them unconditional love, but even those people can still improve their self-esteem if they want to. How? By looking at yourself honestly, being kind to yourself, practising optimism, and setting goals for yourself.

What contributes to low self-esteem?

If you've had a bad experience with being judged or criticised by other people in your life, that can make you feel insecure about yourself. Another way to lose your sense of self-worth is by comparing yourself to others - this can make you feel less than everyone else because there will always be someone more intelligent or prettier.

We all want to feel good about ourselves, and if high self-esteem means having a positive sense of our worth and value, then who wouldn't want that? But there are problems with having this sort of "positive sense of our worth or value." For starters, what exactly is one's worth or value? Is it how much money we make? Our job title? How many people like us on Facebook? How many followers do we have on Instagram? If you ask a stranger who has high self-esteem, they will say yes. But if you ask them why they have high self-esteem, they probably won't be able to tell you why—it will just be a feeling inside them or something that they assume about
themselves without thinking about it too much.

Self-reflection about your self-esteem

Next, I want you to reflect on what bothers you about your self-esteem. Ask yourself the following questions. Make some notes of your answers.

1. When did I first notice that I had low self-esteem?

2. What is it that bothers me about my self-esteem?

3. Do I believe in myself?

4. What talents do I have?

5. What are my good qualities?

6. When last did I feel good about myself?

7. What happened when you felt good about yourself?

8. Do I constantly compare myself to others?

9. What do I love about myself?

10. How has having low self-esteem affected my life?

Some practical exercises you can implement right now to increase your self-esteem

What practical exercises to increase your self-esteem can you start implementing today?

1. Only surround yourself with people who support you and have the same value system as you during your times away from work when you can control why you are spending time with them. When you make friends, you're looking for like-minded people. You want to be around people who are fun to spend time with, who like the same things you like, and who share your values. The best friendships are those where both people support each other in reaching their goals. That's why you must surround yourself only with people who support your actions. Avoid negative people who say things that make you feel bad about yourself, disrespect you, or never celebrate your success.

2. Belief in yourself. Why is it important to believe in yourself? What do you say to yourself when you wake up in the morning? What do you tell your friends, your family, and your coworkers about what you think of yourself? What kinds of things do you tell yourself about how capable of doing something you are? If what you say about yourself doesn't match up with the qualities you know you possess, then all of those negative thoughts are causing a rift between who you know you are and who everyone else thinks you are. Negativity leads to uncertainty, indecision, and even fear.

3. Spend time on what you like to do and what makes you feel good about yourself. If you want to read the paper in the morning, do so. If you like to help out at the local animal shelter, do that. If you like to jog around your neighbour-hood, get out there and start jogging around your area. If you want to plan weekly menus and shop for groceries every Sunday, go ahead. If you like spending time with friends, call a friend and invite them out for coffee. If you have a passion project or hobby, put some time into it. Whatever makes you feel good about yourself is worth spending time on—in fact, it's time we should all be spending more on our well-being instead of always trying to please others or getting caught up in other people's agendas. We'll never have a perfect life if we're always trying to make other people happy instead of focusing on what we want. Don't get me wrong. I'm not advocating selfishness here—just don't let other people's priorities become your priorities. You will never be happy with who you are if you're constantly being told how to act or what you should be doing with your life by people who

don't know you.

4. Do not compare yourself to others, this puts unnecessary stress on yourself. It's easy to get caught up in comparing yourself to others, especially on social media. Countless "look at this amazing thing my friend is doing" posts, a coworker's vacation photos posted immediately after yours, and the constant pressure to keep up with the Joneses. It can make you feel inadequate and like you don't measure up.

5. Redirecting negative thoughts into positive ones will help you become more confident and build your self-esteem. Challenge negative thoughts - catch yourself when you're having negative thoughts about yourself and challenge them! Think about why those thoughts might be wrong or untrue, then replace them with more confident thoughts that bring you back to a place of peace and pleasure.

6. When we're feeling down, sometimes it's hard not to think of what else could be going wrong, or what else we should be doing—it seems more manageable and more productive to focus on the things that aren't working out. But this kind of thinking can do nothing but make you feel worse while letting the opportunities for growth and happiness surrounding you slip by. We all have negative thoughts from time to time, but sometimes they can be so overwhelming that we cannot focus on anything else. If you find that you can't stop thinking about the same things over and over again in a negative way, it's time to learn how to redirect your thoughts into more positive ones. Whether it's a bad day, a rough week, or an uncertain future you're worried about, your thoughts

are spiralling out of control. Don't worry—you're not alone. Everyone has negative thoughts from time to time. It's just how our minds work—but when they start to take over our lives and make us feel like we can't control them, it's time to take action.

7. Become more aware of the good things about yourself. Are you kind and generous? When you notice good qualities in yourself, such as being a kind person or being able to sing well, it can make you feel good about yourself. When you think about how good you are at something, you are thinking about something positive about yourself, which can help you feel better about yourself.

8. Find out your strengths and remind yourself of these strengths throughout the day. Refer back to it when you need a boost in confidence. Keeping this list handy will remind you of everything that makes you unique and strong. Maybe when you don't feel like doing something, you can look at this list and decide if the task is worth doing anyway because your strength might help you accomplish it well. Or maybe looking at this list will give you the courage to improve something in your life because it will remind you of all the things that need improvement.

Using lofty questions to reframe how you think about yourself

The last section for today is to reframe how you think about yourself. You can instill new ideas in your subconscious mind by asking the specific questions below.

Find a quiet place where you will not be disturbed. As an optional option, you can also use the Kubera Mudra while asking the questions (you don't have to if you do not wish). Join the tips of both hands' index finger, middle finger, and thumb. Curl the ring and little fingers toward the palm's middle.

Be as calm and peaceful as possible. Now repeat the following lofty questions as many times as possible while holding this position with both hands:

- Why do I always believe that I am enough?

- Why am I always at peace with myself?

- Why do I always know that I am powerful and confident?

- Why do I always deserve to be happy?

- Why am I always proud of myself?

- Why do I always appreciate who I am?

- Why do I always choose to view my life positively?

- Why do I always value myself as a person

- Why am I always kind to myself?

- Why do I always enjoy the present moment?

- Why do I always love myself?

- Why am I always worthy of love?

- Why do I always believe in myself?

- Why is there nobody else like me?

- Why am I always perfect just the way I am?

Perfect, use these lofty questions often whenever your self-esteem is low. You will notice a gradual shift in how you perceive yourself. Make some notes about how you feel after you have repeated the lofty questions

How do you feel after today's challenge?

What has resonated with you the most?

Day 2: Working On Your Self-Confidence

On day 1, you worked on your self-esteem (the way you see yourself). Today, you will be working on your self-confidence (how you think other people see you based on your self-esteem), which builds on day 1. What is self-confidence? Self-confidence is the belief you have in your abilities. It tells you that you can do anything you set your mind to and helps you to accomplish it.

Self-confidence helps you to believe in yourself, your decisions and choices and is especially vital when it comes to making decisions you can handle and making a decision that will benefit you. It is like a shield that protects you from harm and helps you to feel good about who you are.

Too often, when we think of self-confidence, we associate it with work accomplishments and social status. But in reality, being confident is more than just having a high position in your workplace or knowing how to network. It's about believing in yourself and your ability to take on new challenges and feel good about your decisions.

Self-confidence is vital for your success and happiness in life. Have you ever known someone talented and capable but never tried anything because they didn't think they could succeed? This person won't be happy with their life because they aren't achieving anything or even trying to achieve anything. Self-confidence also boosts your self-esteem, which makes you feel better about yourself; the reason why having low-self esteem can also affect your confidence.

Your low self-confidence can be caused by a variety of circumstances, including but not limited to:

- Growing up in an environment that was primarily unsupportive and critical.

- Experiencing separation from friends or family for the first time.

- Evaluating yourself too harshly.

- Being terrified of failing.

People who lack self-confidence are more likely to make mistakes and have negative self-talk. When your self-talk is positive, you are likely to be more successful. However, when many of your childhood memories are negative, your self-talk stands in the way of your success affecting new opportunities and your quality of life.

Lack of self-confidence is terrible for many reasons. If you lack self-confidence, you won't try new things because you're afraid of doing something wrong. A lack of self-confidence can also hurt your personal and professional relationships. People will notice if you don't believe in yourself or your abilities. When it comes to your relationships, people want to spend time with those who are confident because confident people are fun to be around. Confident people are more likely to be successful in relationships because they are more comfortable and less likely to doubt what others think about them. They also tend to be happier overall, making them more attractive companions.

Successful people are confident because they know what they want out of life and how to achieve their goals. They clearly know what they want and how to get it.

Self-reflection about your self-confidence

Next, I want you to reflect on what bothers you about your self-confidence. Ask yourself the following questions. Make some notes of your answers.

1. When did I first notice that I have low self-confidence?

2. What happened when I saw my lack of self-confidence?

3. What is it that bothers me about my confidence?

4. Is my self-talk primarily negative?

5. What do I say to myself that is negative?

6. Am I always worried about what would happen?

7. How do I present myself to others when I first meet them?

8. Do I know what I want in life?

9. Do I know myself, my unique qualities?

10. How has having low self-confidence affected my life?

Some practical exercises you can implement right now to increase your self-confidence

I believe that self-confidence is an essential skill for everyone to have. It allows you to feel more confident about yourself, your abilities, and your future; it helps you make decisions and take chances, and it can help you achieve success in many areas of life.

There are many ways to improve self-confidence, and here are some easy suggestions:

1. Take a break from your mobile phone or computer. Much of our self-image comes from how we believe others see us online. If you want to increase your self-confidence, step away from social media for a while. You'll be surprised just how much better you look without that filter!

2. Your posture has a direct impact on how others perceive you. Keep your chin up, shoulders back and head high, and don't slouch. Not only will this make you look taller, but it also makes you appear more confident. Walking into a room with confidence is a skill you can learn. It's not something that happens; it takes more than just putting on your favourite outfit.

3. Facial expressions are necessary for conveying to others how you feel—and the same goes for your body language. If you

keep your arms crossed or tucked away in your pockets, people will assume you're closed off from them. Instead, keep your arms open and relaxed, and stand with good posture so that people can see that you're confident in yourself.

4. Live in the present. When you worry about something that will happen, there's no way you can solve the problem or prevent it from happening, so why give it any thought? Instead, it would be best to focus your energy on creating new experiences in the now, increasing your self-confidence even more. The more self-confident you are, the easier life becomes because you are less likely to dwell on what might go wrong in the future or fret about things from the past.

5. Consider all that you have already accomplished. If you believe you haven't achieved anything, you quickly lose confidence in yourself. Create a list today of all the accomplishments you've had in your life that you're pleased with, such as completing high school with a good grade or becoming proficient in a new
language. Keep the list close and add to it anytime you accomplish anything that makes you proud. Whenever you feel insecure about yourself, please take
out the list and use it to remind yourself of all the fantastic things you've accomplished in the past.

6. I cannot stress enough that a positive mental attitude toward your capabilities and strengths is the foundation of self-confidence. It indicates that you have a sense of control over your life and accept and trust yourself. You have a healthy awareness of your capabilities and limitations and a constructive

outlook on

who you are. You can manage criticism, set objectives and goals that are reasonable, and communicate assertively.

7. Don't listen to people that don't have your best interests at heart or tell you something just because they want to hear themselves talk or because they think it will make them look good by comparison. Instead, listen to people who care about your opinion and take steps towards making it a reality. Listening to others will help guide your decisions and make you see if they are right for you or not.

8. Surround yourself with positive people--the people around you cannot help but reflect your feelings about yourself. Choose uplifting and supportive people. It is crucial to unfollow people on social media who make you feel bad about yourself.

9. Knowing who you are and what you want is the most critical step toward more self-confidence. Knowing who you are can identify what makes you happy, what kind of lifestyle you want to live and how much money it costs.

10. Smile more - When you smile, it makes others feel good, and it makes you feel good as well.

11. Make sure to take care of yourself. Therefore, get enough sleep and eat right.

12. Get out of your comfort zone--try doing something new each week. Challenging your comfort zone will stretch your skills and make you feel good about accomplishing some-

thing new!

13. Listen to upbeat music, especially songs that lift rather than bring you down.

14. Be careful how you speak to yourself. Focus on positive self-talk instead of negative self-talk.

Using lofty questions to reframe how you think others see you

The last section for today is to reframe how you think others see you (linked to your self-esteem). You can instil new ideas in your subconscious mind by asking the specific questions below.

Find a quiet place where you will not be disturbed. Now slightly bend your index finger and place your thumb between the first and second knuckles of your index finger. Spread out your third, fourth, and pinky fingers. If you do this with both hands, it will be even more potent (this is known as the Ahamkara Mudra).

Be as calm and peaceful as possible. Now repeat the following lofty questions as many times as possible while holding this position with both hands:

- Why am I always enough?

- Why is my value not diminished by my imperfections or the perceptions of others?

- Why am I always deserving of good things?

- Why am I always deserving of happiness?

- Why am I always stronger than my fears?

- Why am I always in complete control of my emotions?

- Why can I always achieve everything I want?

- Why am I always grateful for everything I have accomplished?

- Why am I always stronger than I think?

- Why do I always learn something new from every experience?

- Why do I always deserve to feel good about myself?

- Why am I always kind to myself?

- Why is every day an opportunity to do better?

- Why do I always have the right to feel confident?

- Why do I always never compare myself to others?

This brings us to the end of day two's challenge. Use these lofty questions often whenever you need more self-confidence. You will notice a gradual shift in your confidence. Make some notes about how you feel after you have repeated the lofty questions.

How do you feel after today's challenge?

What has resonated with you the most?

DAY 3: ATTRACTING MORE POSITIVITY INTO YOUR LIFE

D ay 3's challenge is about attracting more positivity into your life.

Why do some people have a negative outlook on life? I've known people who seem almost to relish that things won't go their way. They always see the glass as half empty instead of half full.

If you've ever had a bad day and then tried to think about it later, only to find that you can't remember any of the bad things that happened, you've experienced the power of positivity. Your brain works like a filter, letting in the good while blocking out the bad. It's easy to see why this might be useful—if we could get rid of all the bad stuff, our lives would be perfect! But it's impossible to live without ever experiencing negative things.

If the stress of life doesn't seem worth it anymore and you're tired of feeling down or anxious, being positive might help give your life direction. If you're constantly thinking positively, you're telling yourself that your feelings are manageable, and since they aren't as overwhelming as they once were, it's easier to deal with them calmly. When you feel calmer and happy with yourself, your whole life changes—you have more energy for everything from work and hobbies to relationships with friends and family. You'll even get sick less often when you're positive!

According to research and self-help gurus, negativity is a state of mind that can affect us in more ways than we realise. Figuring out how negativity operates in our day-to-day lives is not always an easy task, especially if it's something you're unaware of. But there are clues. For example, studies show that negative people are not very good at reading social cues in others. They tend to have difficulty interpreting the meaning behind facial expressions or body language, which affects their relationships. If someone is always finding fault with other people, this is a red flag. They risk losing sight of the good in those around them and being left out of meaningful relationships. Negative people also tend to be less physically active and have a higher risk of obesity.

Furthermore, negativity is a kind of stress, and stress has been linked to everything from indigestion to diabetes. Chronic stress can make you sick in a lot of ways. A study by the American Psychological Association revealed that 77% of people experience at least one type of stress-related health problem in their lifetime, and 42% have experienced two or more issues. Stress has been implicated as a cause of such diseases as heart disease, anxiety disorders, depression, fibromyalgia, and digestive disorders. Not only does being negative affect your mental health, it can also negatively affect your physical health.

Negativity can also be contagious. The mere presence of a negative person can bring everyone else down around them as studies have shown. It's like the old adage about misery-loving company: if you're surrounded by negative people all the time, you will start feeling bad too.

Just as negativity can bring you down emotionally and physically, positivity can help you feel better overall. You can uplift your mood in many ways every day—and if you're feeling low enough that you need some outside input to get back on an even keel, there are plenty of resources.

The key is finding realistic ways to make your life more positive daily, which means doing things you enjoy each day. These things can be reading a good book or listening to uplifting music. Positive thinking is a tool that can be used to improve your life in many different ways, and it can help you to be happier. This tool is excellent for any situation, whether you are in a good mood or not. To live a better life, you must put yourself in situations where positive things will happen. Being positive about the future can help you to see that there is a better tomorrow.

Have you ever told yourself, "I'm not pretty enough," or, "I'm a terrible person"? Unfortunately, most of us do this. Negative self-talk is a way of thinking that can hold us back from achieving our goals or reaching our full potential. We've all been there, myself included. We all experience negative self-talk, and it can have an authentic effect on our lives. We might tell ourselves that we're not smart enough, attractive enough, or good enough to accomplish what we want to achieve. These feelings can be an obstacle when it comes to attracting success in our lives. Understanding why negative self-talk happens and

what we can do
about it is essential.

Thoughts always come into our minds—some positive and some negative. The real problem isn't that those thoughts occur but that we give them so much weight in our lives. Negative thoughts are just a part of the way our brains work—but when we think about them repeatedly and give them too much
power in our minds, they stop being just thoughts and start becoming a part of who we are.

Self-reflection about your negativity

Next, I want you to reflect on what bothers you about your negativity. Ask yourself the following questions. Make some notes of your answers.

1. When did I first notice that I am always negative?

2. What happened when I saw how negative I was?

3. What is it that bothers me about my negativity?

4. Is my self-talk primarily negative?

5. What do I say to myself that is negative?

6. Do I always expect the worst to happen?

7. Why do I always anticipate the worst to happen?

8. What are my first thoughts when I wake up in the morning?

9. What do I have in my life for which I can be grateful?

10. How has being so negative affected my life?

Some practical exercises you can implement right now to become more positive

There are several things you can do to attract more positivity into your life:

1. Recognise your negative thoughts for what they are: thoughts. You don't need to fix, judge, or even analyse why they're popping up right now. You need to take a step back from the thought and recognise that it might not be the entire truth and that you see only parts of the issue.

2. Think of positive thoughts that you want to carry with you throughout the day, and repeat them to yourself in the morning while you're getting ready and throughout the day when it comes up— whether it's something as simple as "I am enough," or "Today will be a good day."

3. When life feels overwhelming, take some time away from it all—even if just for an hour—and focus on an activity that makes you feel happy (for example, reading or cooking).

4. You can't think about two things at once, so when you're going through a tough time or feeling lost, focus on what you're grateful for which can go a long way.

5. Remember that a positive attitude is about making realistic assessments of the world around you and then using those

insights to help yourself and others. It is a powerful tool that can help you in your day-to-day dealings with the world around you, and it's also a great way to stay happy even in the face of stress or disappointment.

Using lofty questions to reframe your negative thinking patterns

The last section for today is to reframe your negative thinking patterns. You can instill new ideas in your subconscious mind by asking the specific questions below. Find a place that is quiet with no disturbances. By intertwining your index fingers, which stand for the element of air, you can imagine anything you want to "let go" of just being blown right out of your system and out of your fingertips (this is known as the Kshepana Mudra). This Mudra is an effective visualisation technique for releasing negative emotions.

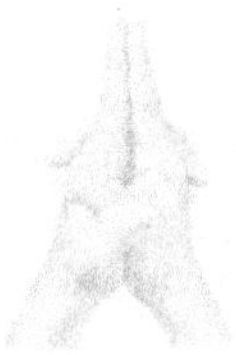

Be as calm and peaceful as possible. Now repeat the following lofty questions as many times as possible while holding this position with both hands:

- Why am I always free of my negative thoughts?

- Why do I always release everything in my life that blocks my growth?

- Why am I never restrained by my thoughts?

- Why do I always choose to release everything that binds me?

- Why do I always breathe freely and openly?

- Why do I always focus on the present moment?

- Why am I always in charge of my thoughts?

- Why do I always choose to change the way I think?

- Why does negative thinking always waste my time?

- Why do I always choose to be happy?

- Why do I always choose to remain positive?

- Why am I always free from any resentment?

- Why do I always choose to set myself free from negative thinking?

- Why am I always filled with positive actions?

- Why do I always transform negative energy into love and light?

This brings us to the end of day three's challenge. Use these lofty questions often whenever you need to feel more positive. Make some notes about how you feel after you have repeated the lofty questions.

How do you feel after today's challenge?

What has resonated with you the most?

DAY 4: RELEASING LIMITING BELIEFS ABOUT MONEY

Today's challenge is about releasing your limiting beliefs about money.

Beliefs are tricky and can be so entrenched in your subconscious that you may not even know they're there. Not to mention there's the fact that they can be challenging to release.

Remember how it feels when you receive any money. You're thrilled because it is like a rush of positive energy. Money is nothing but energy and a universal currency that carries your desires and intentions to the Universe. Think of money as a superhighway, allowing your thoughts and emotions to be quickly transmitted to the Universe.

The idea that money is energy may seem strange, but it's a constructive way to view how people and money relate. When you're stuck in an old pattern of feeling alienated from money, viewing it as something outside of yourself rather than a natural aspect of your being can help shift your mindset.

Believing that it's an impossible task to make more money or manage finances are examples of limiting beliefs. So is believing that debt is inevitable or that making smart investing decisions is only for the rich. These beliefs will hold you back because they keep you from doing what you must do to achieve financial success. They can lead you down a path of financial mediocrity when your potential is much greater.

Why do people have limiting beliefs about money? Because they don't know any better. Most of our parents didn't know how to handle money well, so they passed down their beliefs to us, and it's up to us to surpass those beliefs and learn how to handle money well.

Be aware of negative beliefs about money that may be holding you back from realising your full potential and finding happiness and abundance. Here are some more limiting beliefs:

- Money is the root of all evil

- There's never enough money

- Rich people are greedy

- Money doesn't grow on trees

- The more money I have, the more problems I'll have to deal with

- It's terrible to want things

- I'm not smart enough to make a lot of money

Acknowledging and releasing negative beliefs about money—especially if you're new to a positive-money mindset—can be daunting. It can also seem like it's beyond your control. Today's challenge is about how you can take toward freeing yourself from the grip of these beliefs, which can ultimately lead to a more positive
relationship with money and, consequently, more financial freedom.

Today is an opportunity to take control of your money beliefs once and for all—to decide what you do and don't believe about money, and then to get rid of any negative thoughts that may be holding you back.

Self-reflection about your limiting beliefs about money

Next, I want you to reflect on your negative beliefs about money. Ask yourself the following questions. Make some notes of your answers.

1. How would I describe my general attitude towards money?

2. Do I avoid thinking about my money situation?

3. Do I always feel a lack of money in my life?

4. Is my self-talk about money primarily negative?

5. What do I say to myself about money?

6. What are my first thoughts about money when I have to deal with my monthly expenses?

7. What long-term ideas do I have about money and my future?

8. How has being so negative about money affected my life?

Some practical exercises you can implement right now to change your limiting beliefs about money

Here are some techniques for finding and ridding yourself of any money beliefs that aren't serving you:

Focusing on the why: To change your thoughts about money, you need to take some time to reflect on why you have these beliefs. You might have had a bad experience in the past with money, or someone else made you feel like these things were true. Once you figure out where they came from, it will become easier to change them. Set aside some time to understand why you have limiting beliefs about money.

Focusing on the what: One of the simplest ways to work on your money situation is to change your beliefs about money. The following actions can be helpful:

- Identify the negative ideas/feelings you have about money. If you're having trouble pinpointing exactly why a particular view is pessimistic, writing it down is a great way to help you figure it out.

- Ask yourself what the evidence that these beliefs are true is. You can then examine its truthfulness—is it something that makes sense? Or maybe discuss its thought process—is it built on generalisations?

Focusing on the how: How can you shift your perspective on these beliefs? Is it possible to have a different or more positive attitude towards money? Do the following:

- Look at each belief itself: if you feel you've been carrying around a specific belief for a long time, this belief has likely been accumulating over time. Ruling out the more straight-forward possibilities is helpful to arrive at your particular belief—examine which memories or pieces of advice seem to have been the source of your current
thought process and how you can overcome these.

- Write down more positive thoughts about your money. Consider how you would like to improve your ideas about money.

- Next, list money goals that support more positive beliefs about your money.

Using lofty questions to reframe your limiting beliefs about money

The last section for today is to reframe your limiting thinking patterns about money. You can instil new ideas in your subconscious mind by asking the specific questions below. Find a quiet place where you will not be disturbed. By intertwining your index fingers, which stand for the element of air, you can visualise anything you'd like to "let go" of being blown straight out of your system and out of your fingertips (the Ksepana Mudra which you used previously). This Mudra will also be an effective visualisation technique for releasing your negative emotions about money.

Be as calm and peaceful as possible. Now repeat the following lofty questions as many times as possible while holding this position with both hands:

- Why do I always have enough money?

- Why am I always financially secure?

- Why will there always be more money in my life?

- Why do I always deserve financial prosperity?

- Why do I always have more money than I need?

- Why is there always abundance everywhere around me?

- Why are my bills always paid on time and in full?

- Why is my financial situation always getting better and better every day and in every way?

- Why is money always my friend?

- Why am I always an excellent money manager?

- Why do I always have the power to be a financially successful person?

- Why is my life always full of wealth beyond money?

- Why do I always believe in my ability to use the money that comes into my life to meet my financial goals?

- Why do I always believe in my ability to earn more money?

- Why do I always choose to spend my money wisely?

- Why do I always have the ability to build a base of financial literacy?

Now also repeat these lofty questions with the Kubera Mudra position.

This brings us to the end of day four's challenge. Use these lofty questions often whenever you need to overcome your limiting beliefs about money. Make some notes about how you feel after you have repeated the lofty questions.

How do you feel after today's challenge?

What has resonated with you the most in terms of your personal finances?

Day 5: Change You Way You Think About Your Health

Day 5 is all about changing the way you think about and prioritising your health, including paying attention to issues that cause too much stress in your life. Perhaps you consider your health unimportant and don't prioritise your well-being because you are working too hard or struggling in other areas of your life.

It would help if you cared about your health because it's your most important thing. Health is wealth. Even though you may have all the money in the world, you will be very poor if you don't have good health. That is why today focuses on making your health your number one priority.

You're only healthy when you have a strong immune system, enough energy to get through each day, and when you can think clearly. And when you have a poor diet and don't exercise, the rest of the things in your life will suffer because of it. It's not just that you'll be overweight or out of shape—you could be putting yourself through unnecessary stress, with long-term consequences for your body and emotional well-being. If you never take care of yourself, it will take some effort to change your ways, but it's well worth it.

Stress is the main reason why people get sick. Our bodies are not made to handle too much stress and start showing signs of wear and tear. Stress can make you feel tired, have headaches, have trouble sleeping, and even kill you. The primary stress hormone, cortisol, suppresses your digestive and reproductive systems, growth processes, and immune system responses. Cortisol is also responsible for stopping functions that, in a fight-or-flight scenario, might be damaging or unnecessary.

In today's modern society, stress is handled differently than in other centuries. Also, our stress comes from our jobs, responsibilities, relationships, school and the daily grind. We have deadlines at work to meet, bills to pay, traffic jams, relationship drama and other issues that can affect us mentally, physically and
emotionally throughout our lives. It's hard for us to find time for ourselves or relax, which is why stress has become a significant health problem in
today's society. Bad health affects your quality of life in many ways. It can cut down on the amount of time you spend doing what you love and what you want
to do and how much energy you have to do it.whether you are running a marathon or just trying to get through the day.

Especially stress makes us sick and is the number one health problem for many people. You can't live a healthy life when you are constantly stressed out.

Another problem is that there are many negative beliefs about health. For example, some people think that getting enough sleep is not essential and that they must be productive until the early morning hours. Others believe that they need to be slender to be healthy, which can lead to an eating disorder and can happen to anybody.

While it is hard to reverse this kind of thinking, today will be all about taking that first step to becoming healthier.

Self-reflection about how important you consider your health and well-being

Next, I want you to reflect on the importance of your health and well-being. Ask yourself the following questions. Make some notes of your answers.

1. How would I describe my general attitude towards my health?

2. Am I feeling happy? Why? Why not?

3. What does self-love mean to me?

4. Am I always stressed?

5. Do I always feel tired?

6. Do I take care of myself?

7. Do I prioritise my health?

8. Do I have healthy eating habits?

9. Do I put aside some time in the day to relax?

10. Do I sleep enough?

11. Do I drink enough water?

12. What do I love about my life?

13. How can I improve my mental health starting today?

Some practical exercises you can implement right now to change how you think about your health

Try the following which you can implement right now that will set you on a path to better health:

Always start by being honest with yourself: What needs to change? Please take a moment to make an appointment with a doctor or other health practitioner or ask somebody who knows you well what lifestyle changes they think might benefit you. Then, prioritise what's most important right away. You might want to consider starting small—take a walk every day or meditate each morning, for example, and then work up from there. The steps don't have to be huge at first; they need to be something different from what you've done in the past. And if you find that one change isn't enough, don't worry. Keep making minor improvements until you're where you want to be.

Most people don't know that having an open mind can help them improve their health. This mindset accepts new ideas and tries to learn from them. People with this mindset can see different points of view and take in information that might be contrary to what they know or believe. They are also more likely to be creative and come up with new ideas. You should therefore try out different things and make decisions based on your experience rather than sticking to one path because it feels safe or predictable. It also means you should try not to judge something before you experience it for yourself, as this will limit your growth potential. It's not always easy to change, but it's possible. It takes courage and determination to start something new, and it can be tempting to give up on the first obstacle. But if you're open-minded about your recent lifestyle change, you'll have better chances of success.

It is time to make self-care part of your daily routine. Self-care is an integral part of our lives. It helps us to feel better and more energised. But how do we make self-care a daily routine? Plan your week and include some self-care activities in your day to make self-care a daily routine. Then make them a
priority. Some self-care activities could consist of the following:

- Take care of your body by eating healthy, exercising, drinking water and getting enough sleep;

- Focus on the present moment to be mindful;

- Spend time with friends and family;

- You can also express gratitude for everything that you have.

- Taking a few deep breaths will clear your head.

- Make time for yourself by getting a manicure or walking in nature.

You can do different things to practice self-care every day. The most important thing is to find what works best for you and make it routine. Self-care is essential to one's mental, emotional, and physical well-being. It is an integral part of self-love. The benefits of practising self-care daily are numerous:

- Feeling calmer

- Managing stress better

- Improving sleep quality

- Feeling happier overall and being more productive at work or school

Start taking steps to deal with your stress. It is crucial to know what causes stress in your life and how to avoid it. Some things in your life can make you feel more stressed. These include workload, lack of sleep, financial problems, family problems, work-life balance, etc.

First, identify the primary sources of stress in your life so that you can take steps to reduce them. If you have a lot of work to do, you need to prioritise tasks and delegate some tasks to others. If you feel like you have too much work, taking a break or walking might be a good idea. If you are feeling stressed out
because of a lack of sleep, ensure you get enough sleep every night.

Why not start listening to music such as Schumann Resonance? Listening to Schumann's Resonance music is said to have a calming effect on the listener. The most famous frequency of Schumann Resonance is 7.83 Hz which has been linked to alpha brain waves, a state of relaxation and meditation. Make this music part of your daily routine and start noticing the changes.

How does this work? As humans, we're tuned into a specific frequency of electromagnetic energy known as Schumann Resonance. It's the same frequency that's generated by lightning strikes and earth currents, and it's been around since the beginning of time. In the past few years, more studies have been done on the effects of this electromagnetic energy on our health, specifically concerning our brain waves. The results are incredible: Schumann Resonance music (SRM) can help us connect with our innermost selves and naturally bring our brain waves to the same frequency. That's why SRM is so beneficial for meditating, healing, sleeping...and waking up! It's believed that people can even use SRM for cleansing and grounding.

Schumann Resonance music is naturally occurring background music that you can play anytime you need a quick boost or if you want to relax. And because it uses natural frequencies from Earth instead of synthetic beats, there aren't any side effects—it's safe to play as much as you like.

Schumann Resonance music has been linked to various health benefits in preliminary studies. Here are some great health benefits of Schumann Resonance music:

- Helps you sleep better

- Improves your focus

- Reduces stress

- Calms your nerves

- Balances your emotions

- Enhances your cognitive ability

- Improves your mood.

We all know the old saying: good health is wealth. But how often do we hear that phrase and consider what it means? So often, we only focus on a paycheck—not to mention the idea that money is easy to spend and hard to save. But beyond the necessities of food, shelter, clothing, transportation, and health insurance, there's something much more valuable here: your life. Your ability to enjoy this new year depends on living well for many years. The better shape you keep yourself in today, the more fulfilling experiences you'll be able to take part in tomorrow—and for years beyond that. Health isn't just about living longer; it's about living with more energy and spirit than you ever thought possible.

Using lofty questions to change how you think about your health

The last section for today is to reframe how you think about your health. You can instill new ideas in your subconscious mind by asking specific lofty questions below. To avoid interruptions, go somewhere peaceful. Today you will use the Prana Mudra while asking the lofty questions. The word "prana" means "life force." Prana Mudra is mainly connected to your heart and soul and is often used to treat illness. Use both hands to make the Prana Mudra sign. The tips of your little and ring fingers should touch the side of the thumb. The remaining fingers on your hand should be extended horizontally in front of you straight. Align your spine, head, and back to make them stronger. While doing the mudra, you should take deep, steady breaths. At the same time, breathe in and out.

Why am I always grateful for my body?

- Why do I always love and respect my body?

- Why do I always feel peaceful and grounded?

- Why is my mind always at peace?

- Why does it always feel good to take care of myself?

- Why is my body always healthy and strong?

- Why does self love always come easy to me?

- Why am I always worthy of good health?

- Why do I always treat my body with the love and kindness it deserves?

- Why do I always have faith in my own healing?

- Why am I always a priority?

- Why am my food choices always balanced and healthy?

- Why do I always invest time in nurturing both my body and

mind?

- Why do I always listen to what my body is telling me?

- Why am I always open to new ways to improve my health?

This brings us to the end of day five's challenge. Use these lofty questions often whenever you need to work on your health. Make some notes about how you feel after you have repeated the lofty questions.

How do you feel after today's challenge?

What has resonated with you the most in terms of how you prioritise and think about your health?

DAY 6: ALLOWING MORE ABUNDANCE INTO YOUR LIFE

Well done with coming this far. I hope you will revisit the previous exercises as often as you need them.

Today you must start to allow more abundance into your life. Most of the time, when we think of abundance, we think of money. But it doesn't have to—and often, it shouldn't. Abundance is a state of mind, a general feeling of having more than you need. It's not just about making money, although improving your financial situation can be part of the process. It's about feeling secure and knowing that your needs will be met in the future, no matter what happens. When you're focused on abundance, you look for the good in every situation and believe that opportunities always come your way. In many ways, it's an attitude adjustment away from being a victim or feeling like you're always at the mercy of outside forces.

The most crucial part of today's challenge is deciding what abundance means to you and practising ways to be abundant in important ways. Different people have different ideas about what it means to have abundance. Most of the time, when we think of abundance, we think of money. For some, it means living in a way that they have everything they need without worrying about money. To most people, it's probably not about having a considerable amount of money. Many people feel they don't have enough money even if they earn a high income. Abundance could mean living without financial worries, though. It could mean being able to pay for the things you want and need without having to wait for them or skimp on them. For some people, abundance could also mean being able to give back to others and assist people who aren't as blessed as we are.

Therefore, it is essential to remember that abundance is not an amount of something but a quality. In other words, you can have a lot of money and still feel like you don't have enough. But if you look at it as a quality, it's possible to be abundant in one area of your life, not another. For example, suppose you have many friends but cannot adequately support yourself financially. In that case, that doesn't mean you're abundant in friendship or lacking in finances – it just means that you're abundant in one area and not the other. Abundance doesn't have to mean money, either. It's a state of mind that can apply to any area of your life. One way to increase your abundance is to make sure your mind focuses on what you do want instead of what you don't want. For example, if you want more money and feel like you're lacking it, notice what thoughts run through your head when the subject arises. Do you think about how little money you have? Do you wish for more? Or do you tell yourself how lucky you are?

Therefore, having abundance is surrounding yourself with a life full of joy, love and wellness, and the habits that help you reach that point in your life are essential to learn and maintain.

Self-reflection about how you think about abundance

Next, I want you to reflect on abundance in your life. Ask yourself the following questions while making some notes of your answers:

1. What does abundance mean to me?

2. In which area(s) of my life do I have abundance?

3. In which area(s) of my life do I need more abundance?

4. What things do I want in my life?

5. What should I do to attract these things into my life?

6. What gives me pleasure and joy?

7. What may I do even now that will bring me more happiness?

8. What is working in my life right now?

9. What possibilities are there in my life?

Some practical exercises you can implement right now to change how you think about having abundance

There are a few things you can do right now to make your life more abundant:

1. Allowing abundance into your life means that you believe that abundance exists and that you can feel it happening in your own life. There are two things about people who allow abundance into their lives: they're happy and believe in the possibility of it happening. That's it!

2. A more empowering way to think is that with each moment that passes, you're choosing between two options: a) being miserable and b) allowing abundance into your life. For example, you can choose misery at any moment by indulging in negative thoughts about how terrible everything is or by taking action to make your life worse, like quitting your job or breaking up with your partner. The other option is choosing abundance, which can be as simple as noticing something beautiful about your environment, or as complex as building yourself a new career.

3. The truth is that many people who feel unhappy are incredibly blessed—they want their blessings to look like something else. This perspective doesn't diminish the benefits of wealth and security and romance; it just helps us recognise the gifts we already have and how they've already made our lives better. Gratitude practice is applicable here, aiming at helping you cultivate an attitude of thankfulness for what you do have in your life rather than focusing on what you don't have or want to acquire. They're essential in helping you identify and take action toward the things you want to change in your life. You will focus on gratitude on day 7.

4. Improved health: On day five, you have learned how to think differently about your health. Practising the principles learned on this day will also attract abundance into your life by feeling happier and healthier.

5. Counting blessings can improve your outlook and reduce stress, boosting your immune system and decreasing the risk for depression, anxiety, cardiovascular disease and pain. It may seem counterintuitive, but good health is the key to abundance in life. A healthy person is more likely to be doing well at work, making them more valuable as an employee; they'll have more energy to complete tasks given to them, and they'll be able to take on additional responsibilities as necessary. They're also going to feel better about themselves and their place in the world, which leads to greater self-confidence and more opportunities for personal fulfilment. The reason for this is simple: when we're healthy, we're happier. And when people are happier and feel better about themselves, they tend to attract the positive energy that brings them what they want in life. After all, the universe wants us to be happy. Not only that, but good health allows people to do things like go on vacation or travel or spend time with loved ones—all of which add up to a better quality of life overall. Even if you're disabled or can't physically be as productive as you'd like in your day job or business venture, good health means you'll have the energy and motivation to explore other opportunities and find different ways to contribute positively to your community.

6. Improved relationships: Become more compassionate toward others and the people in your life. Making a deep and

lasting shift in your relationship perspective can be easier than you might think. First and foremost, start by considering how you speak to yourself. The words you choose to say to yourself majorly impact how you feel about yourself, how other people see you and how you behave in society. It is, therefore, essential to learn to be compassionate toward yourself as well as toward others. Try not to judge yourself harshly, but at the same time, don't be too lenient on yourself, either. Think of your new habit of kindness toward others as a sort of "compassionate accountability" - a way to hold yourself accountable.

7. I want you to pay attention to what's important to you today. I'm a big proponent of the idea that energy flows where attention goes. But what if you're focusing on things that aren't serving you? How do you change your thoughts and feelings about life so that those thoughts and emotions create space for abundance, rather than keeping it out? When you focus on what you don't want, that's exactly what comes back to you—the opposite of it. For example, if we focus on lack of money, we'll attract even more lack into our lives.

8. Do something you love. It's cliche, but it's simple, too. When we're doing something we really enjoy, time goes by quickly. Before you know it, you'll find yourself reaching the end of the day with much more done than you expected. Even if you do something you love only once a week, it will boost your mood.

9. You must be willing to receive abundance. But what does that mean, exactly? It means lowering your guard and allow-

ing yourself to be vulnerable to the possibility that abundance is a reality. What's the worst if you allow yourself to receive abundance? You can always say "no" if you don't like it, or if it doesn't feel right. The important thing is to look beyond money and material things for the abundance you truly want. Your life doesn't have to be about the abundance of money—it could be about abundance in love, friends, or even just an abundance of opportunities. Are there ways you're already receiving more than enough in your life? What do you already have that brings you joy? Start looking for those things instead of focusing on how much more you could have. And remember: when you set your intention on having something else instead of appreciating what's already in front of you, it's easy to start obsessing over what you don't have instead of enjoying what's already there.

Using lofty questions to change how you think about your abundance

The last section for today is to reframe how you think about abundance. By asking specific lofty questions below, you can instill new ideas in your subconscious mind about abundance in your life.

Become as calm and peaceful as possible. If you wish, you can use the Kubera Mudra again while asking the following lofty questions.

Now repeat the following lofty questions as many times as possible:

- Why am I always aligned with the energy of abundance?

- Why am I always open to receiving abundance in my life?

- Why am I always feeling so happy and blessed?

- Why do I always accept and receive unexpected money?

- Why does prosperity always flow easily towards me?

- Why am I always magnet to an abundance of love?

- Why am I always abundant in mind, spirit, and body?

- Why am I always proud of what I've become?

- Why am I always taking care of my health?

- Why do I always know great things are on their way?

- Why am I always full of ideas to make each day a successful day?

- Why do I always open myself to endless possibilities?

- Why do I always use every moment of my life wisely?

- Why do I always have more than enough?

- Why am I always happy with who I am and can be?

This brings us to the end of day 6's challenge. Use these lofty questions often whenever you need to feel more abundant. Make some notes about how you feel after you have repeated the lofty questions.

How do you feel after today's challenge?

What has resonated with you the most in terms of allowing more abundance into your life?

Day 7: Counting Your Blessings - Being Grateful

Welcome to the last day of your 7-day challenge. Today we focus on being grateful. Gratitude is giving thanks for the good things that happen to you. It can also be a feeling of appreciation or happiness about someone or something. Gratitude will change how you think because it helps you focus on what's positive in your life. It also allows you to focus on what's positive in your life. Although your life might not be perfect, there are many things to be grateful for.

Gratitude is an emotion that can be used as a coping mechanism in difficult times. It's not just a feel-good emotion but also a cognitive process that helps you bounce back from challenging situations. It can help people struggling with addiction or depression to focus on the little things they do have instead of what they don't have - which is an essential step in getting better.

People who say "thank you" more often are more likely to feel happy and satisfied with their lives than those who don't practice gratitude regularly.

Being grateful in times of both good and bad is a powerful skill that can help enrich your life in so many ways. Expressing gratitude has many benefits, such as stress reduction and improved physical health. Gratitude is also an essential factor in improving your relationships with other people. The first step toward being grateful is to define what you are thankful for. One way to do this is by keeping a journal or listing things you genuinely appreciate. Some examples could be that you have a loving family, the ability to attend college, or that you live in a wealthy country. Your list can include anything, from big things such as travelling to small things like having water and food to eat daily. This part can be difficult because it requires honesty about everything you take for granted every day. Once you have created your list, try to focus on those items daily; this could mean reading them aloud, meditating on them, or writing about them in your journal. You can even try taking time each evening before sleeping to reflect on the items on your list.

When we think about being grateful, we tend to zoom out and feel the big things in life, like being thankful for our health, family, and friends. And those things are undoubtedly important, but we don't usually associate gratitude with the smaller parts of life that make us who we are.

Gratitude also has the following benefits:

- Boosts your mental strength and sense of self-worth.

- Increases resilience and empathy.

- Allows for better sleep.

- Helps people form good habits.

- Increases happiness and calm.

- Helps you reach your financial goals

- Lets more people know who you are.

We all know happiness is not just about having money or being slim. Even when bad things happen, we can still be happy. Similarly, we can also be unhappy when we win the lottery or become famous. What makes us happy and sad is how we perceive situations, which results from how we think.

Self-reflection about how grateful you are

Next, I want you to reflect on being grateful for what you have in your life. Ask yourself the following questions while making some notes of your answers:

1. What does being grateful mean to me?

2. What are the things I can be grateful for in my life?

3. What are the relationships in my life I can be grateful for?

4. How can I practice gratitude every day?

5. What have others done for me for which I can be grateful?

6. Which relationship in my life am I most grateful for the most?

7. What makes me smile today?

8. What am I looking forward to the most?

9. What aspects about my job/daily routine do I enjoy the most?

Some practical exercises you can implement right now to practice more gratitude

At some point in our lives, we're all told to be grateful for what we have. It's a simple idea that is often hard to put into practice in our hectic, modern life. But with some planning we can all find time for gratitude and reap the benefits, namely better health, increased happiness and positive relationships. Being grateful is a fantastic way to be happier and healthier, but figuring out how to be more grateful can seem daunting. Here are some easy exercises you can start doing right now to find more things in your life for which to be thankful:

1. The first step in practising gratitude is to reflect on what you have in your life right now. The self-reflection questions in the previous section will be helpful. Don't think of this as a chore or something you must do, but rather as an exercise to help you appreciate what you already have right now. Look around you, literally and figuratively, and ask yourself if there are things you take for granted daily that are important to you. For example, family members, friends, people who put up with your misbehaviour at work or school, hobbies that keep you sane during stressful times, and books that provide comfort when you're feeling down. If we look at our lives from this micro perspective, there is always something to be

thankful for. And if you think about it and make a list of all the important people in your life, like your kids, parents, siblings, partner, spouse, best friend, or pet(s), you should be thankful for the love they show you every day.

2. Think about the good things in your life by keeping a gratitude journal or talking with friends about what they're grateful for. Write down at least five things you are thankful for each day.

3. Do something nice for yourself—treat yourself to a hobby you enjoy or a meal at your favourite restaurant, and then be grateful for that experience.

4. Have some gratitude for "appointments." You don't want to stop thinking about gratitude once you've gotten yourself into practising it—you need to keep up the positive feelings. That's why having regular self-reflection sessions about what you are grateful for will keep you on track. Schedule these appointments in your diary.

5. Include "gratitude minutes" in your daily routine—a 60-second pause where you reflect on something for which you are grateful. This can be about anything, from how you feel to the beautiful bird you saw in your garden.

6. Feeling grateful is a way of life. And I'm not talking about the "I'm so grateful I have a smartphone" kind of gratitude. I mean feeling grateful for what you have experienced in your life. If you're naturally pessimistic or cynical, try to take on an attitude of gratitude every day. Even if it's only for a few minutes at a time, try to get your mind off the bad things and

back on the good ones.

7. Listen to gratitude meditations on YouTube. There are many meditations available. I like the gratitude meditation by Mary Kate.

Using lofty questions to change how you think about gratitude

The last section for today is to reframe how you think about gratitude. By asking specific lofty questions below, you can instil new ideas in your subconscious mind about gratitude in your life.

Become as calm and peaceful as possible. If you wish, you can use the Anjali mudra while asking the following lofty questions. You may also be familiar with the prayer hands position, the Namaste position, or just pressing the palms together. There's a high likelihood that you have shown gratitude and dedication or greeted someone with this clear hand stance at some point.

Now repeat the following lofty questions as many times as possible:

- Why am I always grateful to be able to count my blessings every day?

- Why do I always appreciate all the things my wonderful body allows me to do?

- Why do I always give thanks for each exquisite moment?

- Why am I always thankful for the ability to learn, develop, and grow?

- Why am I always grateful for everything good that awaits me today?

- Why am I always grateful for every little thing that brings me joy?

- Why am I always grateful for who I am and everything I am capable of?

- Why am I always grateful for all the lessons I learned?

- Why am I always grateful for the present moment, right now?

- Why am I always grateful for my home and for the security it brings?

- Why am I always grateful for the love I am capable of giving and receiving?

- Why am I always thankful for myself?

- Why do I always wake up with a peaceful mind and grateful heart?

- Why am I always truly grateful for all that I am and all that I have?

- Why is every cell of my body always aligned with gratitude?

This brings us to the end of the 7 day challenge. I hope that you have enjoyed this journey to change how you think for a happier and more fulfilling life.

How do you feel after the challenge?

What has resonated with you the most during the challenge?

Bonus Gift Download For Better Habits

Thank you for buying this book. Download the following book as a bonus gift that will help you live the life you deserve by guiding you to change your habits.

Better Habits

https://emilywatsonbooks.com/sdmdownloads/bonus-gift-7-day-ch allenge/

Some Final Words

I hope that the information in this book will be of value to you. I am still amazed at how powerful our subconscious mind is. Please visit my webpage at https://emilywatsonbooks.com for blog posts on personal transformation with your mind including links to my other books. Also follow me on social media (the links are all on my website).

REFERENCES

Chan, YK. 2017. *Empty Your Cup.* Self-published.

Fennell, M. 2016. *Overcoming Low Self-Esteem: A Self-Help Guide Using Cognitive Behavioural Techniques* (2nd ed.). Constable & Robinson.

Ponder, C. 1999. *Open Your Mind to Prosperity.* De Vorss & Co; Rev Ed edition.

Hay, LL. 1995. *The Power Is Within You.* Hay House.

Murphy, J. 2011. *The Power Of Your Subconscious Mind.* Martino.

Peer, M. 2022. *Tell Yourself a Better Lie.* RTT Press.

Neff, K. 2011. *Self-Compassion: The Proven Power of Being Kind to Yourself.* Yellow Kite.

Robbins, T. 1992. *Awaken The Giant Within: How To Take Immediate Control Of Your Mental, Emotional, Physical And Financial Destiny.* Simon & Schuster.